First published 1977
Reprinted 1979, 1981
Macdonald Educational
Holywell House
Worship Street
London EC2A 2EN

© Macdonald Educational
Limited, 1977

ISBN 0 356 05471 3
(Cased edition)
ISBN 0 356 06507 3
(Limp edition)

Made and printed by
New Interlitho,
Milan,
Italy

Editor
Verity Weston

Design
Robert Wheeler

Production
Rosemary Bishop

Picture Research
Elizabeth Ogilvie

Illustrators
Sackett Publishing
Hayward Art Group
Peter Thornley
Temple Art
Peter North
B. L. Kearley
Tony Payne
Dan Escott
Eric Jewell

Consultants
Harry Strongman
Principal Lecturer
in History,
Bulmershe College of
Higher Education,
Reading.

J. C. Holt,
Professor of History,
University of Reading.

The Normans

Patrick Rooke

Macdonald Educational

The Normans

The story of the Normans covers between two and three hundred years. It began about AD 911 when a band of Vikings, settling in France, founded what was to become Normandy. It came to an end in the second half of the 12th century. By then, men from this single French province had conquered England, had made themselves masters of southern Italy and Sicily and had established the new principality of Antioch.

Considering these conquests, it is not surprising that the Normans are remembered for their military achievements. Their knights were admired by all whom they fought. Although not the first to build castles, the Normans were quick to see their value, especially as a means of stopping those whom they had conquered from rebelling successfully.

However, the Normans were not only concerned with war. They showed a skill in government, particularly in Italy. Here they created a state in which Greeks, Latins, Moslems and Jews could live side by side, preserving their own laws, religion and customs.

Under Norman rule many schools were opened, monasteries established and cathedrals and churches built.

We know about the Normans from various sources. One of the most important of these is the many buildings which they left behind. A second is the writings of men who were alive at the time of the Normans. A third source is the Bayeux Tapestry which gives a pictorial history of the invasion and conquest of England by Duke William of Normandy. Between them, these sources help us to build up a picture of what life was like in Norman times.

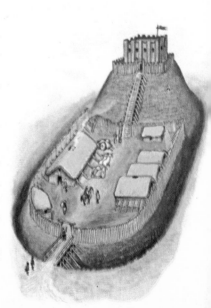

Contents

The conquest of England

On the night of September 27th, AD 1066, a fleet of ships set sail from France to cross the English Channel. The ships were loaded with about 5,000 warriors and their horses, arms and supplies. A lantern burned brightly at the mast of the flagship which carried William, Duke of Normandy, the leader of the expedition. His aim was to defeat the English king, Harold, and win the crown of England for himself.

In the morning of September 28th, William landed at Pevensey but quickly moved on to Hastings where he built a wooden fort. Meanwhile, in the north of England King Harold had just won a great victory, defeating an invasion by the king of Norway. On hearing the news of William's landing, Harold and his tired men at once marched south. They took only eleven days to reach Senlac Hill, near Hastings, on the night of October 13th. The next morning William and his army rode out of Hastings and took up their position on Telham Hill.

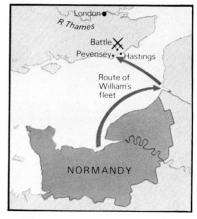

▲ The route of the Norman fleet.

▼ The battle raged all day. Here the Norman army, which included soldiers from other parts of France too, fights its way up the hill towards Harold's lines of foot-soldiers. By late afternoon, Harold lay dead and the English were defeated. On Christmas Day William was crowned king of England in Westminster Abbey.

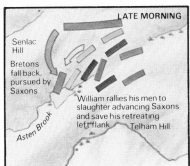

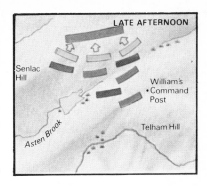

▲ William's archers open the battle with a hail of arrows. As long as Harold and his English army remain on Senlac Hill, they are safe.

▲ The Norman archers fall back and the cavalry and infantry move forward. The Bretons retreat but the English who pursue them are cut to pieces.

▲ Seeing this, William orders his troops to retreat again. The English rush down the hill into the ambush. The Normans launch their final attack.

Who were the Normans?

In the ninth century AD, bands of fierce Viking warriors from Scandinavia attacked and plundered the towns, villages and monasteries of northern France. In 911 the French king, Charles the Simple, in desperation gave some land to a Viking chief, Rollo. The king expected Rollo and his men to defend this land against other Vikings. It became known as *Northmannia*, the land of the Northmen. Later this was shortened to *Normannia*, or Normandy.

The Vikings soon made themselves masters of their new province. They seized the position of lord of the manor from Frenchmen in many villages. Unfortunately we know little about Normandy in the tenth century. But we know that the Viking settlers usually married French women and brought their children up as Catholics. By about 1000 the Northmen were no longer pagan Vikings but French-speaking, Christian Normans.

There are places in Normandy whose names come from Scandinavian words.

Uvetot Criquetot

The ending "tot" is Scandinavian for "homestead".

La Hague

This is from "haugr" which means "hill".

Caudebec

"Caud" meant "cold" and "bec" meant "stream".

Houlgate

The word "gate" meant "road".

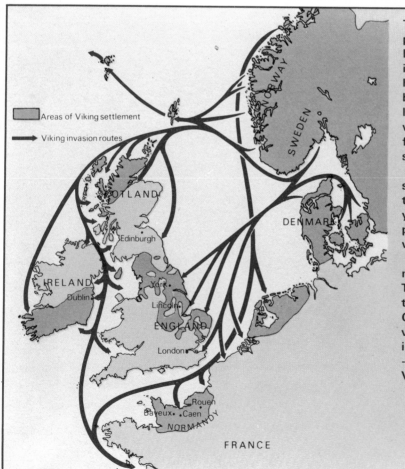

Areas of Viking settlement

Viking invasion routes

The Vikings terrorized the peoples of Europe but later some Vikings settled in the lands which they had once plundered and burned. On this map, the light brown areas show where the Vikings came from and where they settled.

The names of places still sometimes show where these Vikings lived. Above you can see some Viking place names in Normandy with their meanings.

In Britain too there are many Viking place names. The name "Caldbeck" has the same meaning as Caudebec. A town or village whose name ends in -by, -thorpe, -dale or -wick was probably once a Viking settlement.

► William the Conqueror was born in the castle at Falaise in 1027. His father was Duke Robert I of Normandy and his mother was a beautiful peasant girl named Arlette. William was the great-great-great grandson of Rollo the Viking.

The castle's square keep was built in the 12th century but the round tower was added later.

▼ Why did William of Normandy invade England in 1066? The Bayeux Tapestry gives the Norman side of the question. It shows Harold swearing on the bones of saints. The Latin words say: "Harold made an oath to Duke William". William claimed that Harold had sworn to help him become king of England when Edward the Confessor died. Harold denied this and let himself be chosen king.

Adventures in Italy

The Normans made their greatest conquest at Hastings in 1066. But Norman adventurers also had successes in other foreign lands, especially in southern Italy.

At this time Italy was not one country. Parts of it were ruled by the Greek Empire of Byzantium. Sicily had been for nearly two centuries under the rule of Moslem Arabs from North Africa. Therefore there were often quarrels going on between different states or lords.

Many of the first Normans in Italy were armed adventurers seeking their fortunes. They often hired themselves as warriors to one or other of the local lords. Gradually some of them began to win lands for themselves. In 1030 a group of adventurers, led by Rannulf, won land at Aversa, which was to become the first Norman state in Italy. By the end of the eleventh century the Normans had conquered all the large, rich and thickly populated lands of southern Italy and Sicily. This conquest was mainly the work of one family, that of Tancred of Hauteville, near Coutances, in Normandy.

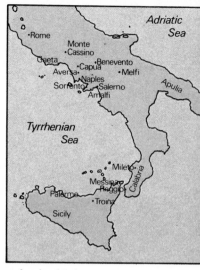

▲ In the 11th century Italy was broken up into many small states. Most were Catholic. A few, like Apulia, were Greek Orthodox. In Sicily the people were Moslems.

▶ The 12th-century church of S. Giovanni dei Lebbrosi in Palermo has Byzantine domes and Norman arches.

▲ Tancred of Hauteville married twice and had twelve sons. He was not rich so his sons could expect little when he died. Eight of them decided to seek their fortunes in Italy.

▲ One son, William, made himself ruler of Apulia. Once, when ill, he was watching his men fight the Byzantines. Suddenly he rushed down the hill and led his army to victory.

▲ Another son, Robert Guiscard (the Cunning), was at one time a cattle thief in Italy. In 1059 he became Duke of both Apulia and Calabria and decided to conquer Sicily too.

▲ Robert's brother, Roger, did much of the fighting in Sicily. One winter, besieged for four months in Troina, he and his wife Judith had only one blanket between them.

▲ The conquest of Sicily lasted 30 years and Roger completed it in 1091. His war against the Arabs there was seen as a crusade, for the Arabs were Moslems by religion.

The Normans in Italy ruled well. They created a state in which Normans, Greeks and Arabs could live together in peace, keeping their own religion, language and customs.

Lords and vassals

When the Vikings came to northern France, they fitted themselves into the feudal system of government which they found there. When, as Normans, they conquered other countries, they developed feudal systems there too. Feudalism was based on the idea that every man had a lord to whom he owed allegiance. He was that lord's vassal and must serve him, for example by fighting for him. In return, the lord gave him land and protection.

Feudalism was closely bound up with land ownership. In England the king was lord of all the land. William I gave about half of England to a few Norman families as a reward for their help in conquering the country. He kept about a fifth for himself and gave the rest to the Church. The people who held land directly from the king were his tenants-in-chief. They had to supply him with knights for his army or pay him a sum of money instead.

Barons
Along with bishops and some abbots, barons were the king's tenants-in-chief.

The king
The king was all-powerful. Although many men owed allegiance to a lord, they all had to be loyal to the king too.

Bishops
Many bishops were as powerful as barons. Geoffrey, Bishop of Coutances in Normandy, had estates in a dozen English counties.

Landless serfs

How wealthy a man was depended on the amount of land he held. Most serfs had no land and were therefore very poor. Serfs were by law not free and many were little better than slaves. Many worked as ploughmen or looked after sheep or pigs.

Villeins

A villein could not leave his lord's land. He held between 15 and 30 acres of land, for which he worked part of each week in his lord's fields.

Cottars

Cottars rarely held more than five acres of land but had to work at least one day a week for their lord. A cottar often lived in a cottage far away from any village.

Freeholders

Unlike a villein, a freeholder did not have to work for his lord. Some freeholders were called sokemen or socmen.

Knights

A knight was a soldier who had been trained in the art of fighting on horseback. William I could call on about 5,000 knights for his army. Most knights held land from one of the king's tenants-in-chief.

Abbots and abbesses

An abbot was head of a monastery, an abbess of a convent. Monasteries held large estates. Like the barons, they had to supply the king with armed knights when necessary.

Important tenants paid homage to their overlord who might be a baron, a bishop or even the king. Kneeling before him, they put their hands in his and swore: "I become your man of the tenements (lands) that I hold of you". They also swore an oath of fealty, or faithfulness, in the following words:

> *"I am your man of life and limb and hereby swear you fealty."*

"How many ploughs?"

In 1086 William I gave orders for a great survey to be carried out in England. He wanted to know about the land and who held it. He believed that many Normans had gained estates unlawfully.

Commissioners, grouped in about eight teams, travelled from county to county. They asked questions such as "How many ploughs are there on this manor?", "How many villeins live here?", "How much woodland is there?" and "How many mills are there?" They also wanted to know who owned the land before the Normans came.

The Commissioners recorded their findings in Latin in what became known as the Domesday Book. Its two volumes can still be seen at the Public Record Office in London. Well over 13,000 towns and villages are mentioned in it.

▼ In England and Normandy the land was divided up into estates called manors. Every manor had a lord and somewhere for him to live.

In many parts of England, especially the Midlands and the South, the farm land was set out in two or three large fields. These were divided into narrow strips. Each villein had a number of strips scattered about the fields so that no person had all the best or the worst land.

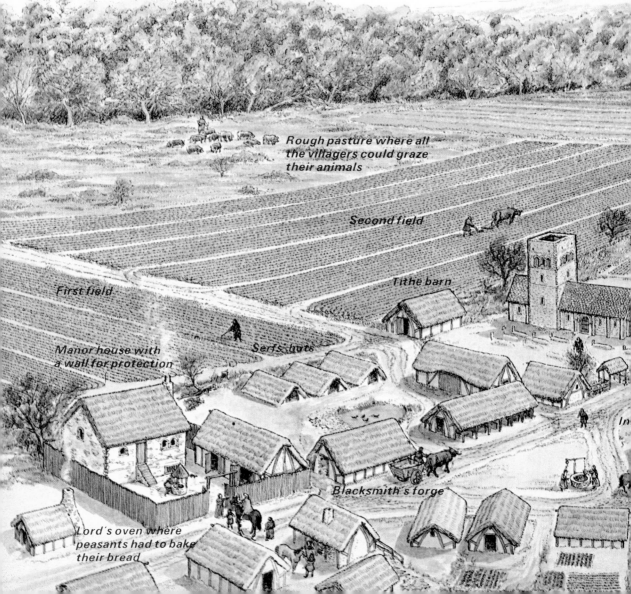

Rough pasture where all the villagers could graze their animals

Second field

Tithe barn

First field

Manor house with a wall for protection

Serfs' huts

Blacksmith's forge

Lord's oven where peasants had to bake their bread

◄ Part of a page from the section of the Domesday Book dealing with Berkshire. The first five lines say: "The king holds Cookham in demesne. King Edward held it. It was then 20 hides but it never paid geld. There is land for 25 ploughs. There are 32 villeins and 21 cottars with 20 ploughs, and there are 4 serfs and 2 mills worth 22 shillings and 6 pence, and 2 fisheries worth 13 shillings and 4 pence, and 50 acres of meadow. There is woodland to render 100 swine and another part of it is in the forest of Windsor".

A hide was an area of land, often 120 acres. Geld was a land tax. The demesne (pronounced "demean") was part of a manor reserved for the lord's use.

Woodland where peasants could gather firewood and feed their pigs on acorns

Third field lying fallow

Villeins' houses

Villeins' gardens

est's se

Lord's water-mill where peasants had to grind their corn

Sheep grazed in the village meadow after the hay had been cut

Ford

Life on a manor

February We can only guess what life was like on a Norman manor, though illustrations like these suggest that it was hard. Winter was particularly bad. There was very little fresh meat, food was generally in short supply and, of course, the weather was cold.

April-May When the spring came there was plenty of work to be done outside. The men, working from daybreak to sunset, were kept busy at such tasks as pruning their apple or pear trees or in planting new ones. The Normans established many new vineyards in England.

August This man is separating the grains of wheat from the straw. This is called threshing. Afterwards the grain was taken to the mill to be ground into flour. The mill was owned by the lord, who also owned the bakery where the flour was made into bread.

October Many peasant women helped in the fields as well as working hard at home. This woman is sowing seed by hand. The seed is probably that of wheat or rye, for these crops were sown in the autumn. Barley and oats were usually sown in the spring.

June A man shears his sheep. Although mutton was a meat that was eaten by the rich, sheep were more widely valued for their wool. This provided the chief material for making clothes. A female sheep, known as a ewe, gave milk from which cheese was made.

July Although this picture shows one man cutting corn, villagers usually worked together at harvest time when crops could easily spoil if drenched by rain. They also combined to share the cost of ploughing, for only a rich man could afford a plough of his own.

November The great advantage of keeping pigs was that they were easy to feed. This man is knocking down acorns for his pig to eat. Pannage was the right to turn pigs into a wood to feed, or the money that a person paid for being given that right.

December After a pig was slaughtered, some meat might be preserved by salting it down. If there was no salt, the meat would be hung in the rafters above the fire where the smoke would preserve it. In Norman times pigs were smaller animals than they are today.

Houses and huts

If you want to discover how wealthy or important a person is today, you may learn a great deal by looking at his house. In Norman times too, a man's house was a good guide to his position in society.

The lord of the manor, or a rich merchant living in a town such as London or Rouen, would probably have had his home built of stone. His house might even have had two floors and several rooms. Many manor houses had their living rooms on the first floor, like the manor house in the picture on page 16. The ground floor was used as a store. Although there were windows, these were just openings in the wall. They might be covered with oiled linen or canvas which kept out draughts but let in some light. Although glass was used in important churches, it was too expensive for use in people's houses.

Most people could not afford houses of stone. They had one-roomed houses made out of mud, straw and wood.

▲ In winter, when he could not work in the fields, a peasant stayed at home and made baskets and wooden spoons, plates and tools. His wife spun and wove the wool from their sheep.

Peasants' huts had no windows or chimneys and must have been dark and smoky inside. Most peasants had very little furniture. They often shared their home with pigs or chickens.

For cooking, peasants used a fire in the centre of the earth floor. At night they slept on a heap of straw, hay or skins.

► This house in Lincoln, known as the Jew's House, is one of the few remaining Norman houses in England. The round arches over the door and windows provide a clue that the house is Norman. The ground floor windows and the window in the roof are from a later period.

The solar, which was a private room for the owner and his family, was on the first floor. Unlike many castles, a house like this usually had a fireplace and chimney.

▼ Peasants built their own houses from materials that were at hand. The simplest house looked like a ridge-tent. Some people tried to improve on this, as in the bottom pictures.

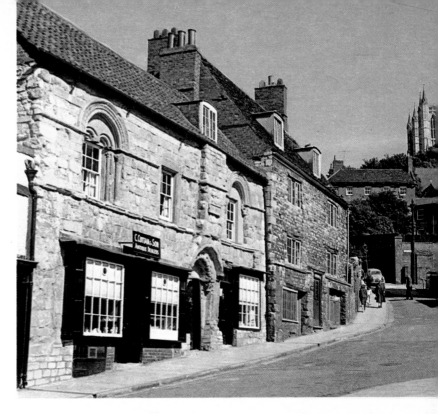

Pairs of wooden stakes were driven into the ground and tied at the top. A pole was fixed along these forks.

More poles were tied across the wooden stakes to make a framework for the house. A doorway was made in one wall.

Small sticks were woven in and out of this framework. Then grass, thatch or turves were added to complete the hut.

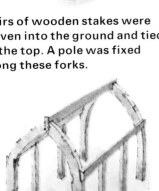

A builder could make a house with more head-room by using a more solid framework of wall posts and cross beams.

The spaces between the beams were filled with wattle (twigs woven together). The wattle was daubed with mud.

The mud dried to produce a hard wall which was some-times painted. The roof was made of rafters and thatch.

Castles

The Normans often had a struggle to hold on to land that they had conquered. Their task was especially difficult in England. Here, with an army numbering only a few thousand, William I had to face many rebellions in the first few years of his reign.

In order to safeguard the new Norman possessions, William therefore ordered castles to be built at important points throughout the country. Many were placed in or near towns to act as constant, grim warnings to the conquered citizens. The Normans often angered citizens by destroying houses on sites where they wanted to build castles. For example, in Lincoln they pulled down 166 houses to make room for the castle.

Many other castles were sited near the south coast to help keep open the sea routes to Normandy.

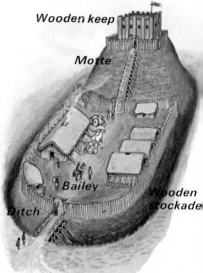

▼ At first, Norman castles in England had two parts: a flattened area called a bailey and a large mound called a motte. Buildings were of wood.

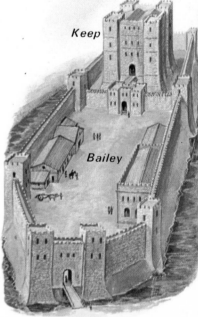

▼ Later castles were built of stone. There was no motte, for the heavy keep had to stand on flat, firm earth that would not collapse.

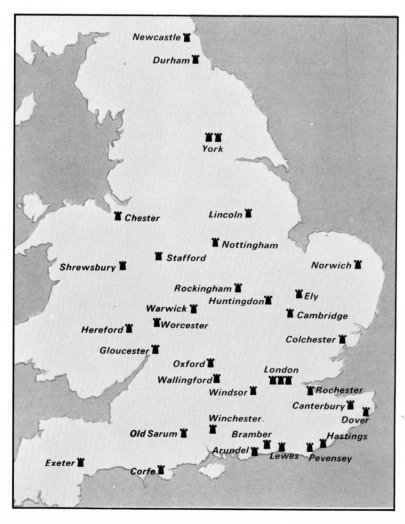

◄ This map shows the chief castles in England built by William I or with his permission.

▲ Sometimes, as at Restormel Castle in Cornwall, builders replaced the wooden stockade around the top of the motte with a high stone wall to produce what was called a shell keep. This one was built in the 12th century, though the buildings inside were added later.

▶ Gisors was once a frontier town in eastern Normandy. Its castle was built to defend the country against the French king who lived in the neighbouring Ile de France. The keep was built in the early 12th century, the wall and towers at the end of the 12th.

Inside a castle

▶ This cutaway picture shows the inside of the stone keep in a Norman castle.

1. A castle could be defended by quite a small force of men. Soldiers kept a lookout from the battlements.

2. There was a chapel in most castles where the lord and his family came to hear mass.

3. The solar, where people are bathing in a wooden tub.

4. The walls might be from 10 to 20 feet (three to six metres) thick. Small rooms were often built into the walls.

5. The lavatory.

6. The great hall, the centre of life in the castle.

7. The armoury.

8. A well was very important for, without a water supply, the people in the castle could not withstand a siege for long.

9. The store-room was kept well stocked with flour, salt, meat, wine, and other foods.

10. Some castles had a dungeon which was used to house prisoners who were awaiting ransom or sentencing.

11. The entrance to the keep.

12. The guard-room.

13. A circular staircase in one of the towers.

14. The cistern, into which rain drained, was a second means of obtaining water.

15. Some towers of a keep were square; others were round.

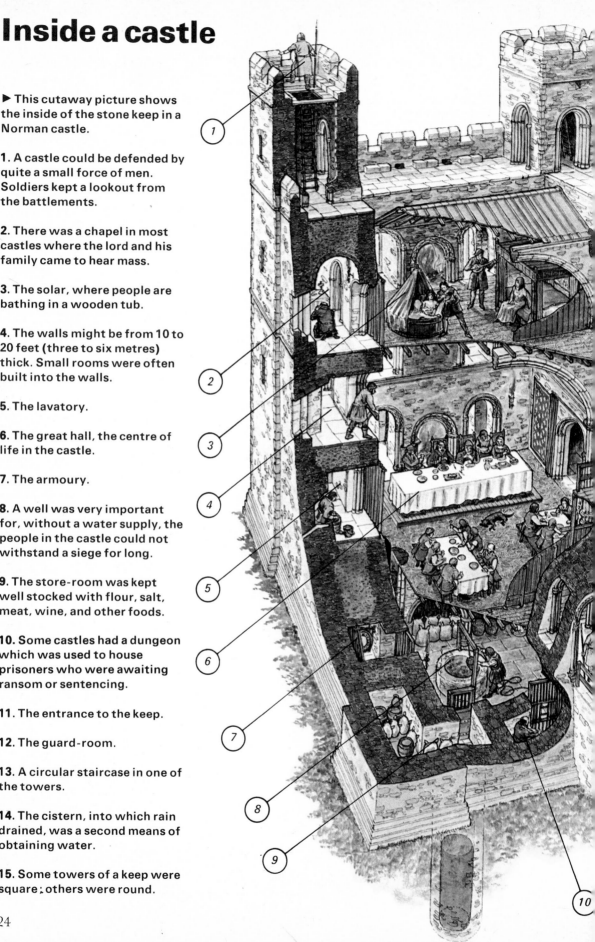

24

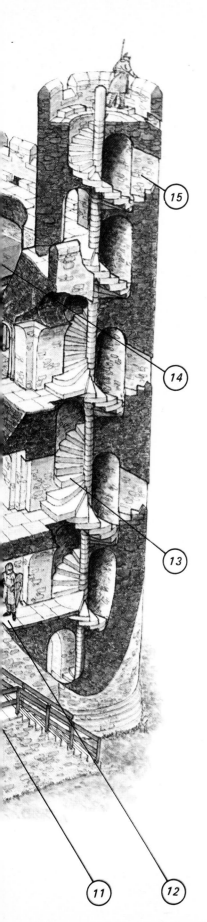

Life in a Norman castle cannot have been very pleasant. People today, used to central heating and electric lights, would certainly have found the inside of a keep much too cold and dark. The great hall was probably filled with smoke. With no proper chimney to the fireplace, there was nowhere for the smoke to escape except into the room. As for lighting, that would have been mainly from rushlights or candles.

The wooden floors were covered with rushes, for carpets did not come into use until later. In some castles tapestries were hung on the walls and these helped to brighten the grey stone. The many small windows of the keep were without glass and, though shuttered at night, were a constant source of draughts.

The great hall was the main room in any keep. It was here that most of the people who lived in the castle, whatever their rank, ate their meals. It was also where many slept at night, either on benches or wrapped in their cloaks on the floor. But the lord and lady would usually retire to the solar, which was an upper, private room. There they slept in a wooden bed which was probably hung round with curtains to help keep the couple warm.

A castle served many purposes. It might be a fortress, a barracks, a place of refuge for nearby villagers, or even be used as a prison.

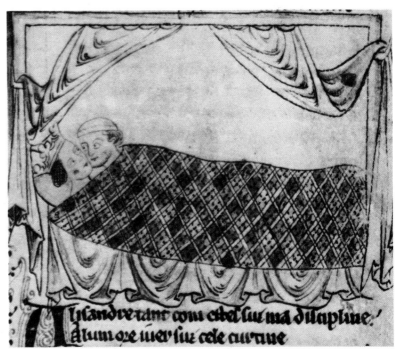

▲ This picture, from a 13th-century manuscript, shows a lord and lady in their curtained bed.

Living in towns

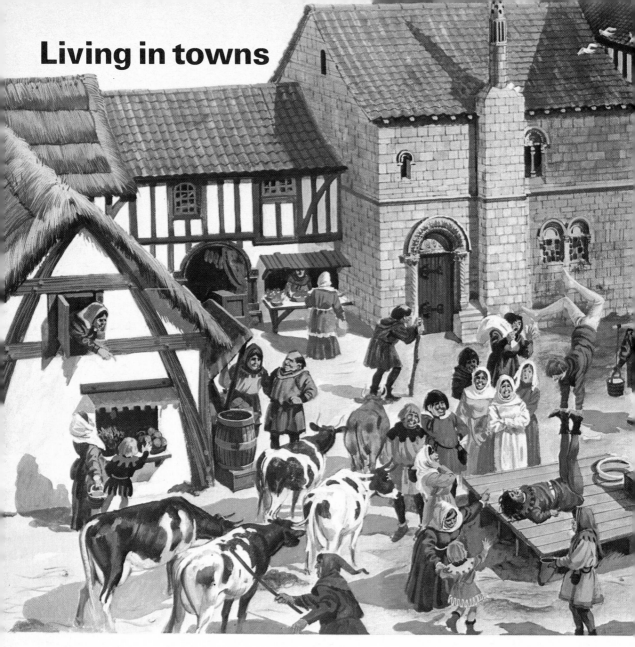

Although towns grew, both in size and number, during Norman times, they were very small by modern standards. London, one of the largest cities in Europe, had a population of only 20,000 at the end of the 12th century.

Feudal lords were keen to benefit from the advantages of having a town on their land. If a lord was able to obtain from the king the right to hold a market, he could lay out streets and offer building plots to traders and craftsmen for rent. He could build a church or two as well and so create a new community.

Disease was a constant threat to all who lived in towns. Rubbish was left to rot in the streets, there was no proper system of drains or sewers and the water supply was polluted. A second danger was fire.

▲ In most towns, as in the one shown here, there were plenty of signs of the countryside. Many people from nearby villages came to town to visit the market which was held in a wide street. Some stopped to look at the stalls or to watch the craftsmen in their shops busily making goods. Others crowded round the acrobats, eager to be entertained. The buildings were mainly of wood, though by the middle of the 12th century a few were of stone.

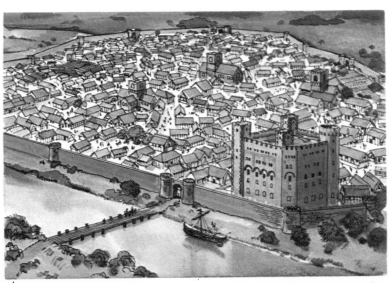

◀ The walled city of London was surrounded by open country. Wharves stretched along its southern side from which merchant ships sailed to many lands. Wool was their chief export and wine the main import, for the Normans were great wine drinkers.

The wooden bridge across the Thames was twice destroyed, once by high winds (1091) and once by fire (1135).

Knights on horseback

The most important part of any Norman army was its knights. We can find out about Norman knights from the Bayeux Tapestry and from other sources such as illustrated manuscripts of the time. These show us what kind of clothing a knight wore and what sort of weapons he carried. The Tapestry also shows the importance of a knight's horse. It pictures horses on board ship, disembarking in England, galloping, charging into battle with their riders and being brought crashing to the ground.

The Normans spent a great deal of time and trouble over the breeding and training of the horses which their knights rode. A Norman cavalry horse, which was specially bred, was called a *destrier.* It had to be strong enough to bear the weight of a rider dressed in mail, yet be able to move at speed when necessary.

The Normans' skill in fighting on horseback helped them defeat the English foot-soldiers in the Battle of Hastings. Their fame as horsemen may explain why the Normans were so much in demand in Italy as mercenaries (hired soldiers). Many of the first Normans in Italy hired themselves out to fight for different local lords.

▼ This small bronze figure, made in about 1150, clearly shows a knight of the time.

◄ A bloodthirsty battle scene from a 12th-century manuscript.

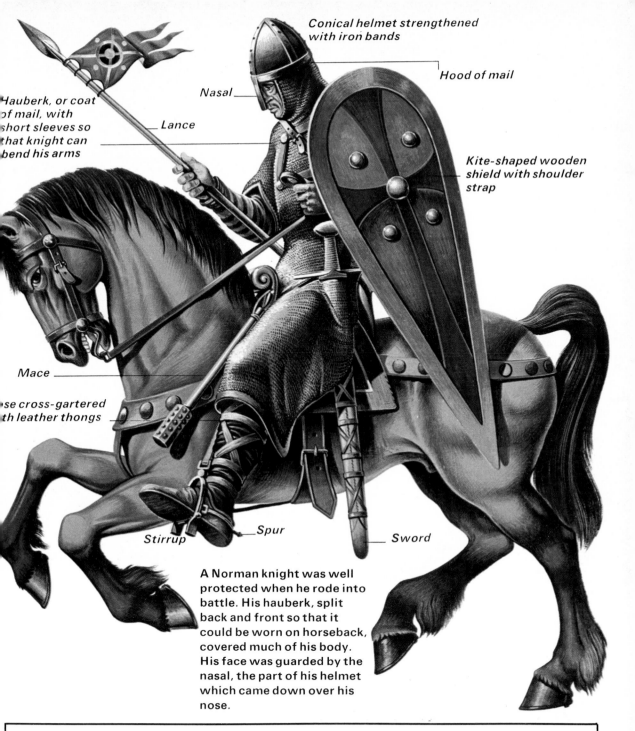

Conical helmet strengthened
with iron bands

Hood of mail

Nasal

Hauberk, or coat
of mail, with
short sleeves so
that knight can
bend his arms

Lance

Kite-shaped wooden
shield with shoulder
strap

Mace

se cross-gartered
th leather thongs

Stirrup   Spur   Sword

A Norman knight was well
protected when he rode into
battle. His hauberk, split
back and front so that it
could be worn on horseback,
covered much of his body.
His face was guarded by the
nasal, the part of his helmet
which came down over his
nose.

Chain-mail is difficult to
make. Lengths of thick iron
wire were wound around a
wooden or metal pole and
then cut into open rings. The
ends of the rings were
flattened and pierced with
holes. Each ring was linked
with four others and then
they were riveted together.

A powerful church

The Catholic Church was rich and powerful. Wealthy men and women, anxious to save their souls, made gifts of money and jewels to churches, so that even a village church might have valuable silver and vestments.

From Rollo onwards, most Norman rulers encouraged the building of new abbeys and churches. They restored others that had fallen into disuse. In Normandy monasteries were restored at Jumièges, Fontenay, Mont-St-Michel and Rouen. Many new ones were built, including the famous abbey of Bec. In England, following the Conquest, the Normans built a great number of churches, monasteries and large, splendid cathedrals.

Leading churchmen held land from the king or duke for which they gave service, just as other tenants-in-chief did. In this way the Norman leaders helped the Church to become wealthy but, at the same time, made sure that its bishops and abbots remained loyal.

The Pope, who lived in Rome, was the head of the Catholic Church. He had the power to appoint all archbishops and bishops. But although the Pope was an important and powerful figure throughout Europe, Norman rulers were not afraid of him. In Sicily it was the Norman Count Roger and not the Pope, who appointed the bishops and archbishops. In England, William I appointed more than a dozen bishops.

▲ This golden candlestick belonged to Gloucester Cathedral.

► William the Conqueror's wife, Matilda, built the Abbaye-aux-Dames in Caen.

▼ One tenth of all produce grown on the manor was taken by the parish priest for the upkeep of his church. This produce was called a tithe.

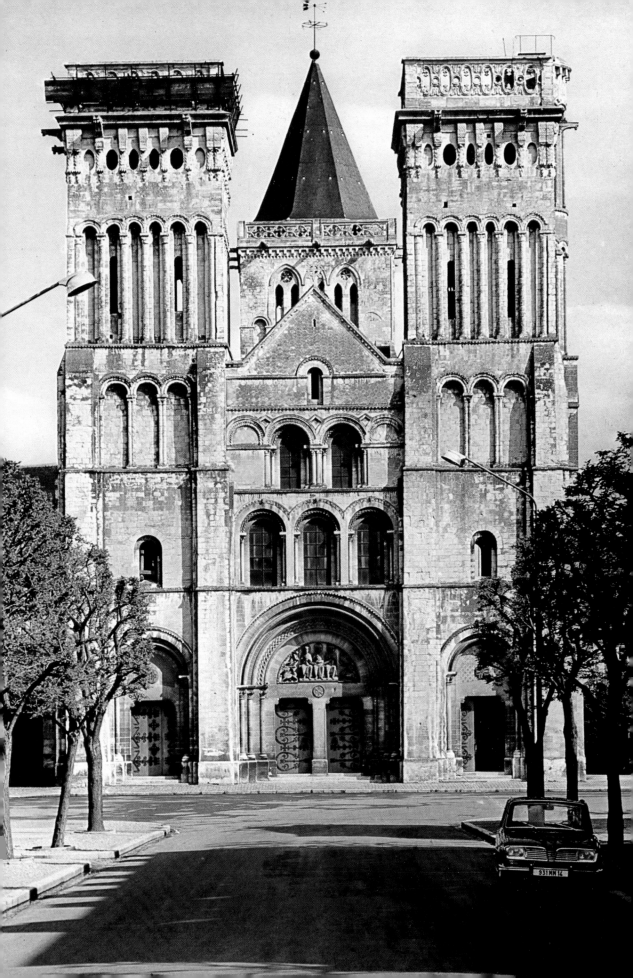

Building a church

The Normans were great builders. During the 11th and 12th centuries workers in stone, wood, iron and glass were busy throughout Normandy, England and Norman Italy. The Normans often gave work to local people, as in Italy and Sicily, where they employed Greek and Arab artists. Today we can still see the results of the labours of craftsmen in Norman times in many of Europe's cathedrals and castles, as well as in thousands of churches.

▲ Glass-makers made a cathedral's windows from pieces of coloured glass joined together by strips of lead. This stained glass window is in York Minster.

◄ There was plenty of work for carpenters to do as most houses in Norman times were made of wood. Carpenters were also needed for the building of churches. While these were usually built from stone, timber formed an important part of the roof and towers.

◄ Smiths were also much in demand. Some iron-workers made swords and other weapons; some produced farming tools. The smiths in this picture are helping towards the building of a church by making the metal tools needed by the carpenters and stone-cutters. They would also have made nails, locks, hinges, bolts and grilles. Most smiths lived and worked permanently in one place.

▲ Stone-masons worked under the guidance of a master mason. They did a number of different jobs. Some dug the stone from quarries. The finest stone came from the quarries at Caen in Normandy. Other masons shaped the stone into blocks and a third group laid the stone blocks. Stone-carvers, like the one on the left, sculpted decorations on the capitals, or tops, of stone pillars.

When a stone-mason had finished one job, he travelled in search of another.

▲ The carved capital of a stone column in the cloister of Monreale Cathedral. The coloured inlay is Byzantine in style. The Cathedral shows us how different styles of architecture were mixed together under Norman rule in Sicily.

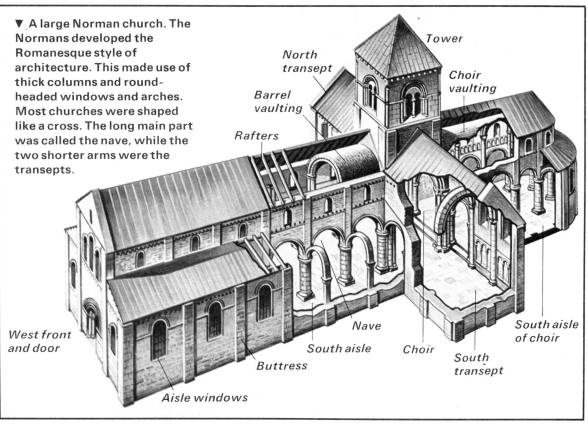

▼ A large Norman church. The Normans developed the Romanesque style of architecture. This made use of thick columns and round-headed windows and arches. Most churches were shaped like a cross. The long main part was called the nave, while the two shorter arms were the transepts.

Tower

North transept

Choir vaulting

Barrel vaulting

Rafters

West front and door

Buttress

Aisle windows

Nave

South aisle

Choir

South transept

South aisle of choir

Monks and monasteries

In the 11th and 12th centuries, religion played a far more important part in people's lives than it does today. Many men became parish priests, while thousands of others gave themselves up to a religious life by going into a monastery. When they entered the monastery as monks, these men gave up all their possessions. They promised not to marry and they vowed to obey the rules of the Order to which they belonged.

Women could lead the same kind of religious life by entering a convent as a nun. There were nearly as many Orders of nuns as there were of monks.

Between 1000 and 1066 the number of monasteries in Normandy rose from five to 30. Much of this increase was due to the efforts of important monks from abroad who settled there. Among the most famous of these was Lanfranc, an Italian. He was Prior at the abbey of Bec and in 1070 became Archbishop of Canterbury.

1. The gate-house.
2. The monks went to the abbey church several times a day. Some great cathedrals began as the churches of monasteries.
3. The *misericord* was a small room where the sick from the infirmary could be given special treatment.
4. The infirmary.
5. The infirmary chapel.
6. The chapter house, where the monks held daily discussions.
7. Dormitories.
8. The cloister, where a monk could walk or read. He might also copy manuscripts here.
9. The refectory or dining-room.
10. The *lavatorium*, where a monk washed his hands before and after meals. There was also a lavatory, or *necessarium*. Many monasteries had running water and drains long before other buildings.
11. Kitchen.
12. *Cellarium* or store-house.
13. The Abbot's house.
14. The Abbot's guest house.
15. House for strangers.
16. Almonry.

Growing up

The chances of a baby surviving and growing up into adulthood were very much less in the 11th and 12th centuries than they are today. Many died at birth. Many others died in early infancy either from disease or from starvation in time of famine.

One cause of death among the very young was rickets. A lack of vitamin D, which is obtained from milk, liver and eggs, causes this disease. The disease is marked by the softening of a baby's bones. It was in an attempt to prevent rickets that most mothers tightly wrapped or "swaddled" their babies in strips of cloth.

Most people lived in villages. In these small communities, it often happened that babies were born to parents whose families were related to each other. This inbreeding was not good, for it could produce children who were physically or mentally weak.

Little was known about the causes of disease. Most treatments were based on the use of herbs, with magic sometimes being tried as well. At times surgery was carried out. This was always brutal and nearly always fatal.

▲ Most schoolmasters believed in using the cane. This illustration, like the others on these pages, is from a manuscript from the Norman period.

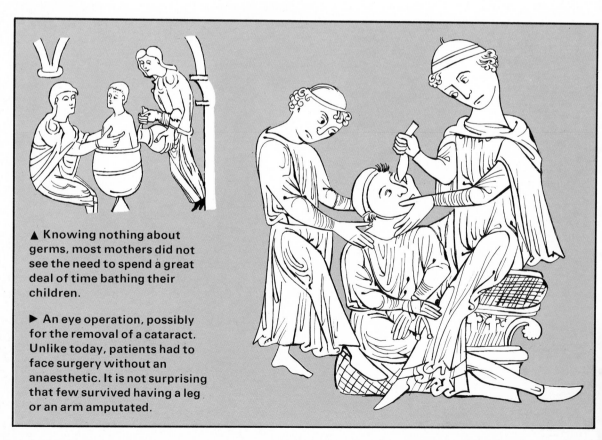

▲ Knowing nothing about germs, most mothers did not see the need to spend a great deal of time bathing their children.

▶ An eye operation, possibly for the removal of a cataract. Unlike today, patients had to face surgery without an anaesthetic. It is not surprising that few survived having a leg or an arm amputated.

▲ A monk writes with a quill pen and holds a knife for cutting the quill. Many monasteries had schools where boys learned to read and write Latin. The Normans spoke French but Latin was their written language, as it was for scholars throughout Europe.

▶ Boys and girls enjoyed playing games. The game of shinty was a forerunner of hockey.

We do not know how many people could read or write in Norman times. There were schools of many kinds, ranging from places which taught basic reading to schools which were the forerunners of universities. But probably only a small fraction of the total population went to these schools. The people who did go were all boys. Girls from wealthy families were taught at home or sometimes in convents. Because they did not spend so much time fighting and hunting, these girls were often better educated than their brothers.

Schools attached to monasteries were mainly concerned with preparing boys to become monks. Other schools, such as cathedral or church schools, provided a broader education. This attracted pupils who would one day seek their living in the outside world, far from the monastery.

Schools were often connected with a particular teacher. The school at the Abbey of Bec in Normandy won international fame when the great Italian scholar, Lanfranc, went there to teach in 1042. He was succeeded by another outstanding teacher, Anselm of Aosta, who unlike other teachers, was against the use of the cane. Both men were to become Archbishop of Canterbury.

▼ This girl seems to be betrothed to one man but another admirer will not give up. Girls often married at 14 or before. The betrothal, when a man and woman agreed to marry, was almost as binding in Norman times as the wedding service itself.

Clothes and hair-styles

▲ The Bayeux Tapestry, which is more than 230 feet (70 metres) long, tells us a great deal about how Norman men dressed. This scene shows a messenger coming to Duke William at Rouen. Notice the hair-styles.

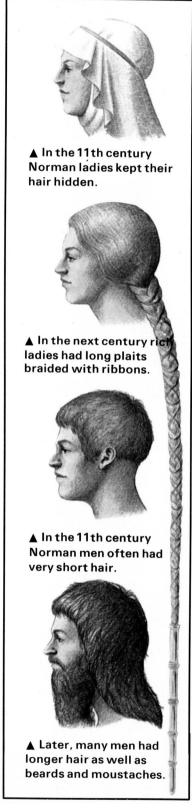

▲ In the 11th century Norman ladies kept their hair hidden.

▲ In the next century rich ladies had long plaits braided with ribbons.

▲ In the 11th century Norman men often had very short hair.

▲ Later, many men had longer hair as well as beards and moustaches.

When a Norman lord was dressing, he would first have put on a *sherte* or *justaucorps,* then a tunic and over-tunic. In cold weather he might have added a mantle (a short mantle was known as a *heuke,* a long one as a *super-totus*). Over all this he might have worn a heavy cloak or *chape.* Long breeches or hose would have covered his legs. On his feet he probably would have worn pointed shoes (*sabbatons*) or soft leather boots (*estivaux*). Garments were generally called by their French names.

For wealthy Normans there were changes of fashion from time to time. This was not so for the mass of peasants who, year in, year out, dressed very simply. A peasant was unlikely to wear a *sherte* and would usually work with bare legs. Instead of leather shoes, he wore wooden clogs, or *sabots.* While the clothes of the nobility were often made from linen, fur or silk, the poor had to make do with coarse materials, such as canvas and skins. All people, rich or poor, relied heavily on the use of wool, though woollen cloth could vary from rough *kersey* to fine *serge.*

How a Norman lady dressed

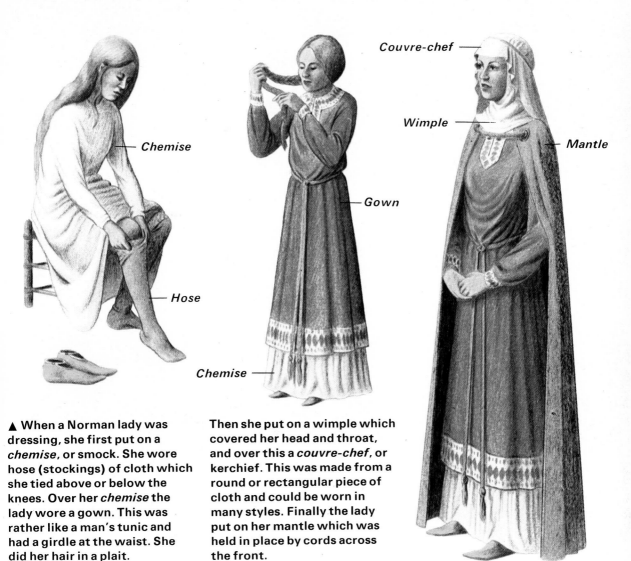

Chemise

Hose

Couvre-chef

Wimple

Mantle

Gown

Chemise

▲ When a Norman lady was dressing, she first put on a *chemise*, or smock. She wore hose (stockings) of cloth which she tied above or below the knees. Over her *chemise* the lady wore a gown. This was rather like a man's tunic and had a girdle at the waist. She did her hair in a plait.

Then she put on a wimple which covered her head and throat, and over this a *couvre-chef*, or kerchief. This was made from a round or rectangular piece of cloth and could be worn in many styles. Finally the lady put on her mantle which was held in place by cords across the front.

Making woollen cloth

Carding. The newly-cut wool was washed, then pulled between spiked boards (cards) until it was free of tangles.

Spinning. The raw, carded wool was put on the top of the distaff and spun, or twisted, by hand onto the spindle below.

Weaving. The spun thread was then woven into cloth on a loom. The cloth was usually about 45 inches (114 cm.) in width.

Feast for a lord

A Norman lord dined in the great hall of his castle or manor house. He sat in a high-backed chair at one end of the large room with his family and special guests. Less important people ate sitting on stools or benches at trestle tables lower down the hall. The lord's table stood on a platform of wood or stone.

The Normans ate their meals off wooden plates or out of bowls. They also used large slices of day-old bread as plates for the meat. Although they had knives and spoons, there were no forks, so most people used their fingers a great deal. Dogs, and sometimes beggars, wandered among the tables looking for scraps.

The lord ate well, even during the winter. Unlike most of the people who lived on his manor, he could afford to buy salt to preserve his meat all the year round. He could also afford pepper to spice tasteless food or food which was beginning to go bad. However, there were certain foods which even a lord might only eat with the King's permission. In England these included venison (meat from deer) and sturgeon (a fish).

A lord's meal included plenty of meat. Beef, mutton, pheasant and heron were very popular. The lord's bread was made from wheat. During a meal the lord and his guests drank heavily of ale and wine.

The peasants' main food was dark rye bread. They grew peas, beans and onions in their gardens and collected berries, nuts and honey from the woods. Peasants did not eat much meat. Many kept a pig or two but could not often afford to kill one. They could hunt rabbits or hares but might be punished for this by their lord.

On the move

Butler in charge of ale and wine

Chamberlain in charge of the King's personal possessions

To travel by land in Norman times could be both dangerous and uncomfortable. Little had been done to repair Europe's roads since they had been built and cared for by the Romans hundreds of years before. Many roads were no more than dusty, rutted tracks when the weather was dry and muddy streams when there was heavy rain.

Because of the bad state of the roads, not many people risked travelling in carriages. The carriages of the time had no springs and so jolted uncomfortably on the rough roads. They might also get stuck in the mud or overturn. Wealthy Normans travelled on horseback; Norman ladies often rode on a pillion seat behind a man-servant. Poor people had to walk. Goods and baggage were transported in waggons or on pack-horses and mules.

A Norman king spent much of his time travelling, inspecting his own scattered estates or visiting the estates of his subjects. He moved from castle to castle, rarely staying in one place for more than a few days. By the time of Henry I, royal visits were often announced well in advance. An English writer of the time tells how each place where the court stopped became like a fair. Merchants and entertainers gathered, eager to make money from the crowds who came to see the King.

Lords who had manors in different parts of the country also travelled from one place to another. Other travellers on the roads included pilgrims, merchants, scholars or even crusaders setting off for the Holy Land.

Most people, however, travelled little. Everything they needed was grown or made in their village and they had no reason to leave home.

▼ A well-padded horse-collar was in use by the 12th century. This was an important invention. Unlike earlier kinds of harness, it did not nearly strangle a horse when it started to pull.

▼ This hammock waggon is shown in an 11th-century manuscript. The vehicle, which had no springs or brakes, was probably only used in or near towns by rich invalids.

Chancellor with
the royal clerks

The King

Noblemen

Steward in
charge of
food supplies

Men-at-arms
for protection

▲ Wherever William the Conqueror travelled, he took a large staff of officials and servants. Probably the most important of these was the Chancellor. As head of the royal clerks, he was in charge of the officials who wrote the royal documents. All records were in the Chancellor's safe-keeping.

Furniture, bedding, cooking utensils and other baggage were carried on pack-horses or in carts.

The problems of moving an army long distances were great. This part of the Bayeux Tapesty shows Normans preparing for the invasion of England. They are busy loading their ships. The hauberks must have been heavy as two men are needed to carry one. The Latin words say: "These men are carrying arms to the ships and here they are pulling a cart with wine and arms". Hundreds of horses also had to be shipped.

Sport and entertainment

How did people with time to spare amuse themselves? William Fitzstephen, writing in the 12th century, says that in summer London's young men might be "exercised in leaping, shooting, wrestling, casting of stones and throwing of javelins". The girls would be "dancing and tripping until moonlight". In winter "great companies of young men" went sporting on the ice.

However, the favourite pastime of the Norman nobles was hunting. Some Norman kings even made special laws and named large areas of land as "royal forests", where no man could hunt without the king's permission. To kill deer and wild boar was a serious crime. Even the cutting of timber was forbidden in land under forest law.

William I cleared farming land and destroyed houses to make the New Forest. A 12th century historian said about it: "This tract of land was thickly planted with churches and with inhabitants who were worshippers of God; but by command of King William the elder the people were expelled, the houses half ruined, the churches pulled down, and the land made an habitation for wild beasts only".

▲ By the end of the 13th century the royal forests covered the areas of England shown here. A royal forest was not all woodland but might include villages and farming land.

▼ The Bayeux Tapestry shows the falcons and hounds which were used for hunting.

▶ Musicians play a zither and a harp (top) and a viol and a horn (bottom).

For people who preferred indoor games, there were chess, draughts, dice and tables, which was a kind of backgammon. A fine set of chessmen, carved in the shape of Norman knights, was discovered in southern Italy.

It seems likely that the Normans enjoyed music, as we have early drawings which shows us various musical instruments that were in use. Horns, zithers, viols and harps were among the instruments known to the Normans. Organs were also in use. Unfortunately, no music has survived for any of the songs which they may have sung.

Short religious plays were popular among both the nobles and peasants. These were sometimes acted in the church itself, or performed outside in front of the West door.

There were also travelling entertainers such as minstrels, acrobats and jugglers. They would perform in taverns, market places or the great halls of castles.

▼ Jugglers were popular entertainers. Jesters, minstrels, dancers, and owners of performing bears were also popular.

Government and law

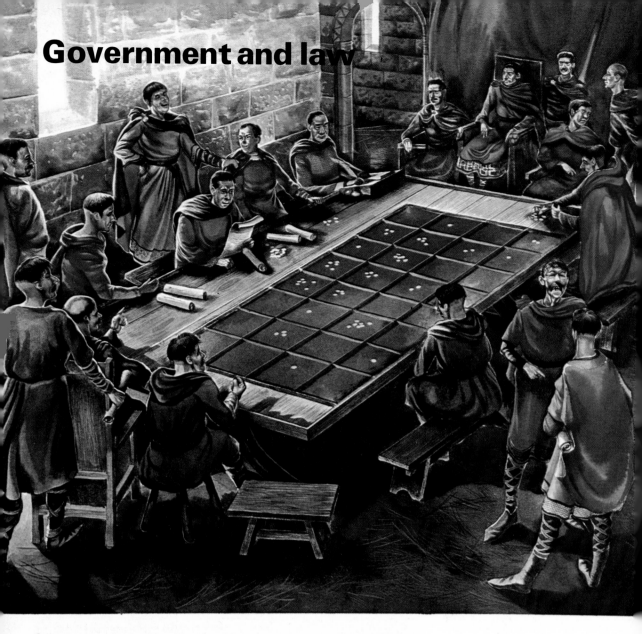

▲ "The Exchequer is an oblong board measuring about ten feet by five. Over this is spread a cloth . . . ruled with lines a foot, or a full span apart. In the spaces between them are placed the counters".
(12th century)

◄ The Witan, shown here, was an assembly that advised Saxon kings. William I replaced it by "great councils" held three times a year. One of the Witan's last acts was to elect Harold as king of England in 1066.

◄ The most common punishments were fines, mutilation and death. It was not until 1166 that Henry II ordered every sheriff in England to have a gaol.

As there were no police, it was not always possible to tell if a person had committed a crime, unless he was caught in the act. The Normans brought a new kind of trial to England. This was trial by battle.

▼ Trial by battle. Two men, the accused and his accuser, fought until one was victorious. By law this one was the winner of the case.

The king's power

When the Normans conquered a country they did not completely change the way that it was governed, nor scrap all its laws. Of course, important changes were made. In England, one of the most important effects of the Conquest was the growth in the power of the king. A Norman law said that every man, no matter from whom he held his land, was the king's man, owing allegiance to the king. Although a lord was responsible for the behaviour of his vassals, whom he could try in his own manor court, men were also brought to trial at the county or shire court. Here they were tried before the sheriff and the local justice, who were officials appointed by the king.

The Exchequer

William the Conqueror used to hold regular gatherings of his tenants-in-chief when he might consult them about the country's laws. For the day-to-day business of government, however, he and his successors relied on special members of his household. One of these, the Treasurer, with his staff, had to collect money due to the Crown and keep the royal accounts. To help them count the money this group used a chequered cloth laid across a table and, as a result, became known as the Exchequer. The Normans were the first to use this system of keeping national accounts.

In Italy it was different. Here the Normans found a land divided into many states, each with its own laws and government. For a time, at least, they succeeded in unifying the south when, in 1130, Roger II was crowned King of Sicily, Apulia and Calabria.

▼ The Durham sanctuary knocker. The right of sanctuary meant that criminals could take refuge in a church, safe from the operation of the law.

The First Crusade

For hundreds of years the Byzantine Empire, with its capital at Constantinople, had been a mighty stronghold of Christianity at the eastern end of the Mediterranean. From the seventh century AD onwards there had been many conflicts with neighbouring Moslems, who followed the religion established by Mohammed. These conflicts grew worse in the 11th century when the Moslem Turks overran Palestine and Syria. In 1095, when Constantinople itself was threatened, the emperor appealed for help. In answer, Pope Urban II urged all Christians to join a great crusade against the "infidels".

This First Crusade was made up of two parts. One, a disorganized mob led by a preacher, Peter the Hermit, was soon destroyed by the Turks. The other was a well-ordered army that included many Norman barons, knights and foot-soldiers.

The most famous of the Norman crusaders was probably Bohemond, the son of Robert Guiscard. Bohemond led the successful attack on the city of Antioch in 1098. When the rest of the crusaders pressed on to Jerusalem, which they captured the following year, Bohemond stayed behind to become Prince of Antioch. He founded a Norman state there which lasted for nearly two hundred years.

A Byzantine princess, who met Bohemond as a young man, wrote of him many years later: "He was so tall in stature that he stood above the tallest. His blue-grey eyes gave him dignity but they could flash with anger"

▲ Many crusaders travelled by sea as well as by land. Norman ships, with their large single sails, resembled those of their Viking ancestors.

▲ The name Saracen was used for any follower of Mohammed living in one of the countries around the eastern Mediterranean. At the time of the crusades it was particularly applied to the Turks, who were fine horsemen.

◀ Nobles, knights and men from every walk of life flocked to answer the Pope's call to arms against the Turks. Normans joined the throng, coming not only from Normandy and England, but, like Bohemond, from Italy as well. The map shows the routes they took.

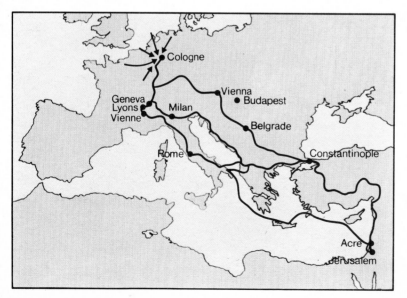

After months spent in besieging the city of Antioch, the crusaders finally captured it by a trick. One evening at sunset they pretended to leave the city, but returned under cover of darkness. By morning, led by Bohemond, and with the help of an accomplice inside the city itself, they were able to launch a fierce, unexpected attack. A bloody battle took place in which large numbers of Turks, including women and children, were massacred. Before long Bohemond's purple banner was flying from the city walls.

A fortnight later Bohemond's entire army came out of Antioch to defeat a relieving force of Turks. This was the greatest single military success won by the Christians during the First Crusade.

▲ This 13th-century picture shows the assault on Antioch. The artist has shown the Normans wearing the helmets of his own time, not those of Norman times. He probably painted the Saracens' faces a greenish colour to indicate his dislike of them.

The Normans disappear

The most puzzling thing about the Normans is the way they disappeared. For two hundred years they influenced the history of Europe in many important ways. During that time historians like Orderic Vitalis and Geoffrey Malaterra made it clear that the Normans, wherever they were living, saw themselves as a distinct and separate people. Yet, by the second half of the 12th century, there had been a change. The Normans thought of themselves as French and English, not as Normans.

It is not easy to know why the Normans lost their separate identity. One reason was probably their readiness to intermarry with other peoples. Robert Guiscard set aside his Norman wife to marry an Italian, while Bohemond of Antioch married the daughter of the King of France. One writer of these times reports that the English and Normans intermarried so much that "it can scarcely be decided who is of English birth and who of Norman".

Many Normans preferred to live on their new estates in England, Italy or Sicily where they were better off than they would have been in Normandy. Some, like Roger II of Sicily, although boasting of their Norman ancestry, had never visited Normandy at all. For much of the time they were prepared to speak the language of the people with whom they now lived and to share their customs. In England they were even willing to share that country's past, sometimes defending their right to property by making use of Anglo-Saxon charters.

The disappearance of the Normans can be dated from a number of events: in England from 1154, when a count of Anjou came to the throne; in Sicily from 1194, when a German ruled; while in Normandy it was 1204, when the country was conquered by the French. Although the heirs of Bohemond continued to rule Antioch into the 13th century neither they, nor their peoples, felt any ties with Normans elsewhere.

What were the Normans like as people? We can get some idea from the writings of historians in Norman times.

"The Normans are a cunning and revengeful people . . . Arms and horses, the luxury of dress, the exercises of hunting and hawking, are the delight of the Normans; but on pressing occasions they can endure with incredible patience the inclemency of every climate and the toil and abstinence of a military life".

Geoffrey Malaterra, an Italian historian of the 11th century.

"When under the rule of a strong master the Normans are a most valiant people, excelling all others in the skill with which they meet difficulties and strive to conquer every enemy. But in all other circumstances they rend each other, and bring ruin upon themselves".

Orderic Vitalis, a half-English, half-Norman historian of the 12th century.

"This King William of whom we speak was a very wise man, and very powerful . . . He was gentle to the good men who loved God and stern beyond measure to those people who resisted his will . . . Amongst other things the good security he made in this country is not to be forgotten—so that any honest man could travel over his kingdom without injury with his bosom full of gold; and no man dared kill another . . . Certainly in his time there was much oppression . . . He was sunk in greed and utterly given up to avarice . . ."

The Anglo-Saxon Chronicle, an English history written from the ninth to the 12th centuries.

The Norman influence

Although the Normans disappeared, they left much to remind us of them. Many of their churches, cathedrals and castles still stand. In England the Old English language, spoken before the Normans arrived, gradually changed as Norman-French words came into it. Some of the developments in law and government which took place in England under the Normans can still be seen today. For example, officials such as the Chancellor, the Treasurer and the Chamberlains who were appointed to assist Norman kings, have their modern counterparts.

During the 13th century Parliament was still unable to make its own laws, but it could ask the king to take certain steps. The king would give his approval to such a request by pronouncing the Norman-French words *le roy le veult*, which mean "the king wishes it". Even today the phrase is used to show the royal assent to any Parliamentary Bill, although with a queen on the throne the words are *la reine le veult*.

▲ In Normandy, England and southern Italy you can still see many Norman buildings. This is the keep of Castle Hedingham in Essex.

Norman-French words gradually came into the English language, but only about 900 are recorded before 1250. These are mostly words which English servants of Norman nobles needed to know. Some examples are: *baron, noble servant, messenger, feast.*

After 1250 the nobles and wealthy people, who had been speaking French since the Conquest, began to speak English. They carried over into English thousands of Norman-French words connected with the church, government, the law, fashion, food, art, and the army. You can see some examples on the right.

Government	*crown, council, reign, state, parliament, rebel, royal, tax, traitor*
Church	*prayer, vicar, baptism, lesson, religion, chaplain, parson, incense, abbey*
Law	*jury, judge, sentence*
Fashion	*petticoat, robe, satin, fur, gown, boots, fur*
Food	*fry, roast, stew, toast, mustard, vinegar, gravy*
Art	*music, melody, embroidery*
Army	*battle, peace, enemy, arms combat, siege, defence, army*

The story of the Normans

AD 911 About this time Vikings, seeking new lands to plunder, sailed up the River Seine. One band, led by Rollo, was invited to settle in the area by the French King Charles, who no doubt hoped that Rollo's men would defend the river against all other invaders. The land where they settled was to become Normandy.

By the early 11th century feudalism was already established, monasteries were flourishing and Rouen and Bayeux were busy towns.

▲ Rannulf founded the first Norman settlement in Italy.

▲ King Charles granted land to Rollo in AD 911.

AD 1030 Legend says that it was Norman pilgrims, returning home from Jerusalem, who first told their countrymen about the fortunes to be made in southern Italy. Before long, men from Normandy were hurrying there either to become hired soldiers or bandits. In 1030 one of these mercenaries, Rannulf, so earned the gratitude of his master that he was given the hill fortress of Aversa, which was to be the first Norman state in Italy. These adventurers were also to include many of the sons of Tancred of Hauteville, the most famous of whom were Robert Guiscard and Roger.

AD 1066 Duke William of Normandy, angry that he had been passed over as king of England by the Saxon Witan, invaded the country and defeated Harold, the Witan's choice, at the Battle of Hastings. William was crowned in Westminster Abbey on Christmas Day as the lawful successor to the English throne.

As he gained control over different parts of England, William shared out the land among his own followers. Therefore, until inter-marriage took effect, society became divided into a ruling class of Norman land-holders and a subject class of English.

In Italy, Robert Guiscard had promised to defend the Pope. In return, the Pope agreed to recognize the Norman as Duke of Apulia and Calabria.

AD 1071 In spite of being recognized as Duke of Apulia, Robert did not actually control all of that territory. Part still remained in the hands of the Byzantine Emperor, who had kept a base in the city of Bari for over 500 years. This long rule came to an end in 1071, when Robert and Roger launched a successful attack on the city.

Within a few months of the fall of Bari, Tancred's two sons set sail for Sicily with a fleet of fifty-eight ships. The port of Palermo was their goal. Roger, who was put ashore with a force of men, crossed the island by way of Troina and set up a blockade of Palermo from the land. Robert blocked entry to the port from the sea. After a siege of some months the Normans took Palermo.

AD 1085

A decisive event took place when, following another siege, a second great port, Syracuse, fell to the Norman invaders. But the conquest of Sicily, which was largely the work of Roger, was not completed until 1091.

Meanwhile, in England, William had managed to suppress most of the opposition to the Conquest and a more peaceful time was marked by the work of the Domesday Commissioners. The record that they compiled in 1086 is known as the Domesday Book. It sets out, county by county, an account of the ownership of each estate in England. It records what each estate was worth, the numbers of people living on it and their status, as well as information about mills, fisheries, pasture, woodland or salt-pans.

▲ Wherever they went, the Normans built strong castles and fine churches.

AD 1098

Of the many Normans who went on the First Crusade no one had a more spectacular victory than Bohemond at Antioch. Whether the capture of this large and prosperous city did much to help the crusaders on their march to Jerusalem seems doubtful. However, Bohemond's action did lead to the setting up of a new Norman state.

▲ Many Normans went on the First Crusade.

AD 1130

When Roger II was crowned king of Sicily, Apulia and Calabria, he became the ruler of a kingdom which was to become, for the next fifty years or so, one of the greatest in Europe. Half-oriental, half European in character, it was rich in learning, government and finance. In no other country could you find men of so many different languages and religions living peacefully side by side.

AD 1154

Henry II came to the throne of England, an event which marks the end of the Norman period in that country, for Henry's father came from Anjou. By the end of the century, not only were the Normans in England ceasing to think of themselves as Normans, but so too were Normans living elsewhere, even in Normandy itself.

Famous Normans

William the Conqueror (1027-1087) became Duke of Normandy when he was only seven. By the time he was a young man he had shown himself to be a brave soldier in many battles. On the death of his second cousin King Edward (the Confessor), William claimed the English throne. Once king, he re-established law and order, taking steps to ensure that the conquered English did not rebel. In 1087, when William was fighting in France, his horse trod on a hot cinder and stumbled, causing the king injuries from which he died.

Odo (1036-1087) was William the Conqueror's half-brother. He became a priest and was made Bishop of Bayeux when only about 19. Odo played an important part in the conquest of England. He paid for many of the ships that carried the Normans across the Channel. Although a priest, he also took part in the battle of Hastings. In return, William made him Earl of Kent and put him in charge of Dover Castle when it was built. It was probably Odo who ordered the making of the Bayeux Tapestry. He died in Sicily when setting out on the First Crusade.

William II of England (1056-1100) was nicknamed Rufus because of his red face. When William the Conqueror died, he left Normandy to his first son, Robert, and England to his second surviving son, William Rufus. Many Normans were unhappy with William Rufus as king, believing that Robert should have followed William I on the English throne. William Rufus was killed by an arrow while hunting in the New Forest.

Robert (1054-1134) became Duke of Normandy when his father, William the Conqueror died. Because he was short and fat, he was nicknamed Curthose, which means "short stockings". In 1096, Robert set out on the First Crusade, returning to Normandy in 1100. In 1106 he was captured by his brother, Henry I of England. He was taken to England and held prisoner there for 28 years until he died.

Robert Guiscard (1015-85) was one of the many sons of Tancred of Hauteville. He followed his elder brothers to Italy and soon won a reputation as a daring soldier. When his brother Humphrey died in 1057, Robert was proclaimed Count of Apulia and shortly afterwards conquered Calabria. He sent Roger, his youngest brother, to seize Sicily, later joining him in the fighting there.

▲ The first four Norman kings of England with buildings they erected. Top: William I with Battle Abbey and William II with Westminster Hall. Bottom: Henry I with Reading Abbey and Stephen with Faversham Abbey.

▼ The late 13th-century figure of Robert, Duke of Normandy, on his tomb in Gloucester Cathedral.

Roger I of Sicily (1031-1101) was the youngest son of Tancred. He was a popular leader, being handsome, clever and brave. In 1057 he joined his brother, Robert Guiscard, in Italy and was soon playing an important part in the conquest of Sicily. When Robert died Roger became ruler of southern Italy and Sicily.

Bohemond the Giant (1056-1111) was the son of Robert Guiscard. He took a leading part in the First Crusade during which he led the successful attack on Antioch in 1098. As a result, that city and the land for miles around became a new state with Bohemond as its Prince.

Roger II (1093-1154) was still a young boy when his father, Roger I, died. Once old enough to rule, he governed with ability and courage. In Sicily he created a state where Christians, Jews and Moslems might live peacefully together. In 1130 he was crowned King of Apulia, Calabria and Sicily.

Henry I (1068-1135) became King of England upon the death of his brother William Rufus, with whom he was hunting at the time. This angered Robert, their elder brother, who was absent on the First Crusade. Robert believed that he had been cheated of his right to the crown. A long drawn-out quarrel followed during which Henry invaded Normandy and took Robert prisoner (1106).

Orderic Vitalis (1075-1143) had an English mother and a Norman father. Although born near Shrewsbury in England, he went to school in Normandy at the Abbey of St. Evroul. Writing in Latin, this Anglo-Norman produced a lengthy history of the Church from the birth of Christ to his own time. This tells us a great deal about life in the times of William the Conqueror, William Rufus and during the First Crusade.

Stephen (1097-1154) was the son of Adela, one of William the Conqueror's daughters. He seized the English throne when his uncle Henry I died, even though the king had named his daughter Matilda as heir. Much of Stephen's reign was troubled by a struggle between his supporters and those of Matilda.

Matilda (1102-1167) was the daughter of Henry I. In 1114 she married the German emperor, Henry V. In 1127 her father persuaded his barons to accept her as his successor but on his death, Stephen seized the throne. In the civil war that followed, Matilda was finally defeated in 1148. She went to Normandy, which her second husband, Geoffrey Plantagenet, the Count of Anjou, had taken. Their eldest son became Henry II of England in 1154. He provided England with strong government, which Stephen, the last of England's Norman kings, had failed to do.

The world the Normans knew

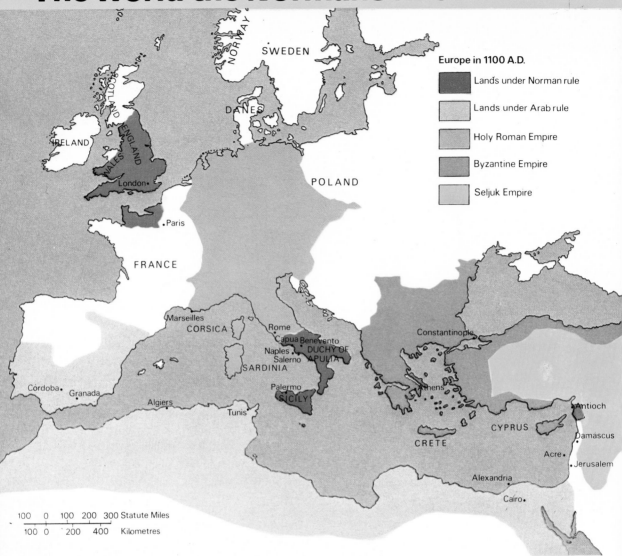

Europe in 1100 A.D.

- Lands under Norman rule
- Lands under Arab rule
- Holy Roman Empire
- Byzantine Empire
- Seljuk Empire

NORWAY

SWEDEN

DANES

SCOTLAND

IRELAND

ENGLAND

WALES

London

Paris

POLAND

FRANCE

Marseilles

CORSICA

Rome

Capua Benevento

Naples

Salerno

DUCHY OF APULIA

SARDINIA

Córdoba

Granada

Algiers

Tunis

Palermo

SICILY

Constantinople

Athens

CRETE

CYPRUS

Antioch

Damascus

Acre

Jerusalem

Alexandria

Cairo

100 0 100 200 300 Statute Miles
100 0 200 400 Kilometres

This map is of Europe in AD 1100. It shows where the Normans settled and established states. Apart from Normandy itself, and one or two small areas in southern Italy, all these Norman conquests were made within the second half of the 11th century.

The Holy Roman Empire, which is also shown, was founded in 800 and was meant to be a revival of the ancient Roman Empire. The rise of Norman power in Italy weakened the emperor, who was no longer able to influence the decisions of the Pope as he had done before. The position of the Pope, on the other hand was strengthened, for he found the Normans useful allies against the emperor.

The Byzantine Empire was the Greek Empire formed when the eastern part of the Roman Empire split off from the western part in AD 395. It was called after its capital Byzantium, otherwise known as Constantinople. Early in the 11th century, southern Italy was regarded as forming part of this empire, though it was too far away to be under very strong control. By the end of the century, the Byzantine Empire was threatened by the Seljuk Turks.

Although William was crowned king in 1066, it was not for some years that he was to win control of all England. He defeated a rebellion in Exeter in 1068. The next year he put down a general rebellion in the north, while in 1071 William at last defeated the troublesome Hereward the Wake in the Fens. A few months later he invaded Scotland and the king of Scotland submitted to him.

SCOTLAND

Edinburgh
Berwick
Carlisle
Newcastle on Tyne
Durham
Richmond
Ripon
Stamford
Bridge
York • Gate Fulford
Tadcaster
Pontefract
Rhuddlan • Chester
Lincoln
Derby Nottingham
Stafford
Shrewsbury
Montgomery
Lichfield
Stamford Crowland Norwich
Leicester Peterborough
Coventry Rockingham Ely Bury
Warwick Huntingdon St. Edmunds
WALES
Worcester Northampton
Hereford Cambridge Ipswich
Brecon Tewkesbury Bedford Colchester
Gloucester Buckingham
Pembroke Hertford
Chepstow Oxford St.
Abingdon Albans
Cardiff Malmesbury Wallingford Westminster LONDON
Bristol Windsor Rochester
Bath Guilford Canterbury
Wells Tonbridge Dover
Old Sarum Winchester
Southampton Bramber Hastings
Exeter Corfe Chichester Lewes
Dorchester Arundel Pevensey
Totnes

10 0 10 20 30 40 50 Statute Miles
10 0 20 40 60 80 Kilometres

ENGLISH CHANNEL

St. Valery

Cap de la Hague
Mortemer
Criquetot
Yvetot
Caudebec Rouen Gerberol
Houlgate Jomièges Gisors
Bayeux Varaville Dives St Clair-
Caen Lisieux sur-Epte
Coutances Mantes
Val-ès-Dunes Bec Evreux
Falaise NORMANDY
Avranches Mortain PARIS
Dol Mont Tinchebrai
St. Michel Sées

Area conquered by 1066

Area conquered by 1068

Area conquered by 1070

57

World history AD 900 to 1200

Normans	Europe	Asia

AD 900

Vikings, under the leadership of Rollo, settled in N. France. At first their new home was known as *Northmannia,* the land of the Northmen, but this was soon shortened to *Normannia* or Normandy. For a time the newcomers no doubt lived much as they had done in Scandinavia.

Athelstan (925-940) was the first king of a united England. The Holy Roman Empire, created by Charlemagne in 800, had broken up. Henry, Duke of Saxony, attempted to mend relationships between the different states, but with little success.

About this time in China wood blocks were first used for printing.
In Japan the Fujiwaras had just made themselves the leadir family in the country.
Buddhism had spread from India to China and Japan.

AD 960

For more than eighty years Normandy was ruled by two Dukes: Richard I (942-96) and Richard II (996-1026). Both encouraged the growth of monasteries. Rouen and Bayeux became important cities. By the end of the tenth century, the people of Normandy no longer thought of themselves as Vikings.

Otto I of Germany and N. Italy reunited the Holy Roman Empire with himself at its head. Pope John XII regretted taking an oath of allegiance to the Emperor so Otto removed him and put Leo XIII in his place.

In China the Sung dynasty (960-1279) came to power under T'ai Tsu. Though he ruled only thirteen years he made important progress in unifying the many states into which Chir was divided.

AD 1020

The Normans made conquests in Italy and Sicily: in 1030 Rannulf established their first settlement at Aversa; in 1059 Robert Guiscard was declared Duke of Apulia and Calabria; and in 1071 Palermo was captured from the Saracens. In 1066 Duke William successfully invaded England and was crowned king.

Brian Boru defeated the Vikings at Clontarf in Ireland (1020). When Pope Gregory VII tried to prevent rulers from appointing bishops, Henry IV, the Holy Roman Emperor became very angry. Gregory banished him from the Catholic Church (1076).

China prospered under Sung rule. The country was efficiently run. Art and science flourished. Kai-feng, its capital, became a thriving manufacturing centre f textiles and porcelain.

AD 1080

The Norman conquest of Sicily was completed in 1091. In the closing years of the century the First Crusade set out for the Holy Land. Among the Normans who accompanied this force was Bohemond. In 1098 he captured the town of Antioch from the Saracens and made himself Prince of a new state.

Another long quarrel between Emperor and Pope about the right to appoint bishops ended in an agreement known as the Concordat of Worms (1122). This gave the right to the Pope. But the argument was far from being settled for good.

Hindu civilization in India reached a new splendour. Unde the Chola dynasty, temples ceased to be isolated buildings and became temple-cities. The Khmers of Cambodia expanded into Burma, Thailand and Vietnam (1128).

AD 1140

Roger II was crowned king of southern Italy and Sicily (1130). His kingdom was to become one of the richest, both in money and in art and learning, in all Europe. Meanwhile England, under the rule of King Stephen, was in a state of civil war.

Thomas Becket was murdered in Canterbury Cathedral (1170). Philip II strengthened the French monarchy. Having quarrelled with King Richard of England while together on a crusade (1190), he returned home determined to drive the English from France.

By the mid-12th century, families other than the Fujiwara had become powerful in Japanese life. Two in particular, the Taira and the Minamoto, ros to prominence.
Genghis Khan became a Mongol leader at the age of fourteen (1174).

AD 1200

	Near East	America	

rica

Near East

America

Africa: kingdom of Ghana (covering ferent area from modern na) was supreme in west a. It was in a position to trol important trade routes. ong the most valuable of the ds which its traders handled e gold and salt.

Near East: The Byzantine Emperor Leo VI (886-912) went to war with the Bulgarians. The long campaign left the Empire's frontiers little changed, but gave control over the Balkans to the Bulgarians.

America: It had been a custom in Maya society to erect carved and inscribed stone slabs to commemorate great events. During the ninth century one centre after another had ceased to erect such monuments.

Fatimids, who claimed cent from Fatima, the urite daughter of hammed, conquered Egypt in and founded the city of o.

The Byzantine Emperor Basil II (976-1025) was determined to avenge his country's honour. In 1001 he declared war on the Bulgarians. The conflict was fierce and long. When a large Bulgarian army was trapped in the Strauma Valley, thousands of Bulgarian prisoners were blinded by the Byzantines.

The Maya civilization continued to decline in Guatemala and Mexico, though in Yucatan it was different. The Maya towns in Yucatan prospered, developing their own style of architecture.

roup of fanatical Moslems, o were followers of Ibn Yasin, ame known as the noravids. In 1042 the noravids embarked on a *jihad* oly war. Before long, they trolled the whole western ert and in 1076 captured the ital of Ghana.

The Byzantines grew tired of war and allowed their army to run down. They seemed unaware of the Seljuk Turks advancing from the east. The Seljuks seized Baghdad (1058), reached the borders of Egypt (1064) and defeated the Byzantines at Manzikert (1071).

By this time the great Maya city of Chichén Itza had become a Toltec citadel. The Toltecs were from Mexico.

hough it is difficult to be tain, the Yoruba Empire bably had its beginnings ut this time. No other African ple have produced so much of high quality as the rubas. This included sculpture wood, clay, brass and ivory.

Alexius Comnenus seized the Byzantine throne at a time when the position of the Byzantine Empire looked desperate. Several times he called to the Pope for help, but it was not until 1095 that any came. The result was the First Crusade (1096-9).

In Peru the Chimu people created a vast coastal empire which stretched for hundreds of miles. Chanchan, the capital, covered about eight square miles. The Chimu built roads and fortresses and had a well-organized state.

adin was Sultan of Egypt. He fered defeat at the hands of crusaders in 1177, but ten rs later Jerusalem surrendered im. Saladin, who died in 93, was a skilful, brave and rciful general.

Further crusades took place. The Second (1147-9) was a sad failure. The Third (1189-92), prompted by Saladin's capture of Jerusalem, had more success, winning for Christians the right to visit that city. Richard I of England and Philip II of France took part.

Semi-civilized tribes, including the Aztecs, poured into the Valley of Mexico and destroyed the Toltec capital of Tula (1168). With the collapse of the Toltec empire, Mexico entered a troubled period.

Glossary   # Index

allegiance loyalty (to king or lord).
bailey the courtyard of a castle.
capital the top part of a pillar.
cloister the covered walk round a square or along the side of a monastery or cathedral building.
cottar a cottager holding only a little land.
crusade an expedition, under the banner of the Cross, to recover the Holy Land from the Turks.
fealty a vassal's promise of loyalty to his feudal lord.
geld a land tax introduced in order to buy off the Danes. The Domesday Book shows that under the Normans not all land was taxed in this way.
hauberk a long coat of mail.
hide a land holding, usually 120 acres, but could be less.
keep the main building of a Norman castle.
kersey a coarse woollen cloth.
manor an estate.
manor court a court held by the lord of a manor or his steward to try cases involving his vassals.
manuscript a book or document written by hand.
mercenary a hired soldier.
motte a mound forming part of many Norman castles.
pannage the right to turn pigs into a wood to feed.
sanctuary a place of safety.
Saracen the name given to any follower of Mohammed living in the Middle East.
serge a good quality woollen cloth.
shire court a county court where cases were tried by the sheriff and local justice.
sokeman a freeman who paid a fixed rent for his land.
solar an upper room.
tapestry a cloth, woven or stitched with pictures, for covering walls.
tenant-in-chief one of the king's vassals, usually a baron, bishop or abbot.
vassal one who held land from, and gave homage to, another.
villein a villager who held between 15 and 30 acres of land. He could not leave his lord's land.